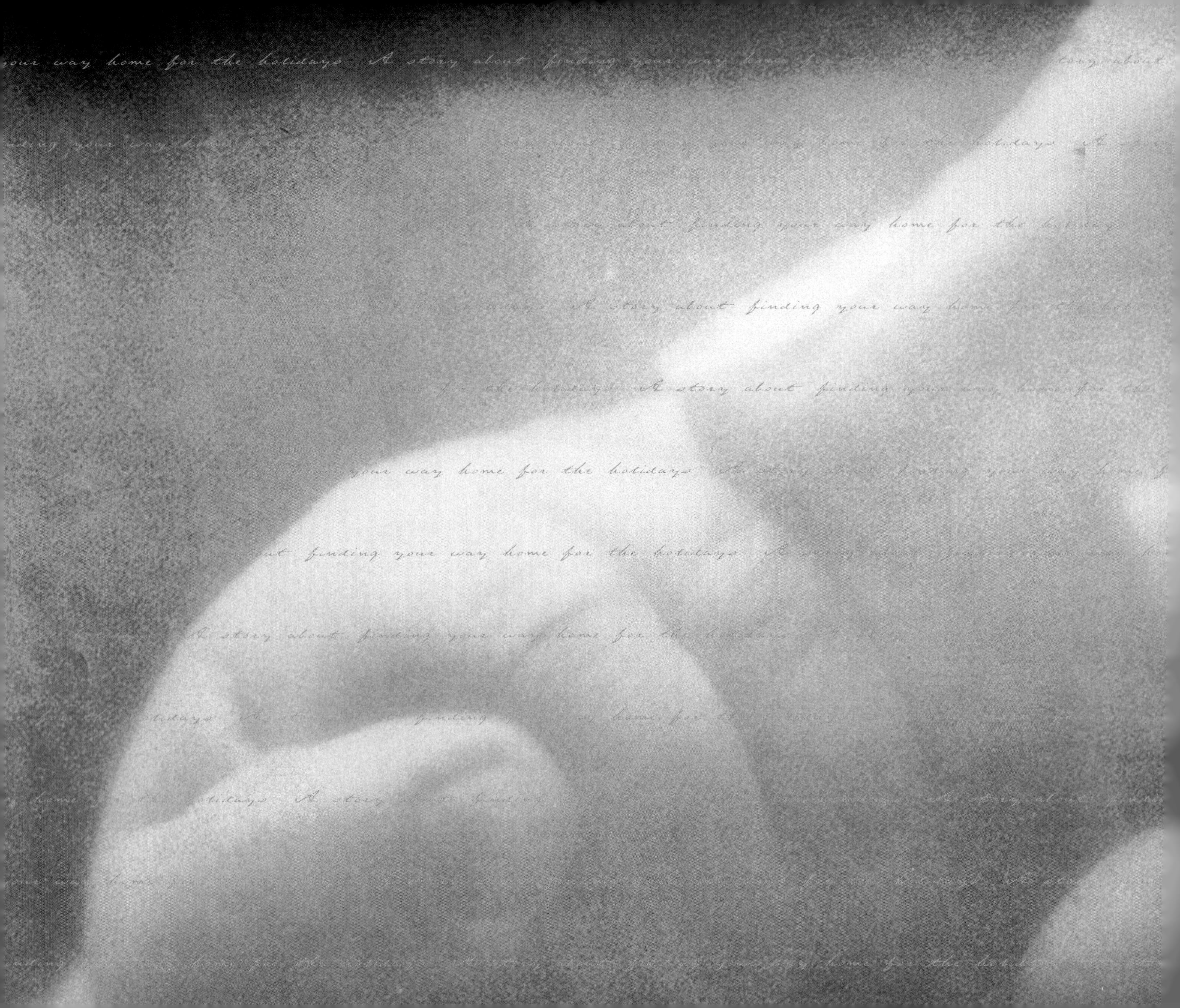

The Christmas CROSS

A story about finding your way home for the holidays

MAX LUCADO

WORD PUBLISHING

NASHVILLE

A Thomas Nelson Company

Published by Word Publishing, Inc. Nashville, Tennessee 37214

Edited by Karen Hill

Photography & Design by Koechel Peterson & Assoc., Mpls., MN

Library of Congress Cataloging-in-Publication Data
Lucado, Max.
    The Christmas Cross : a story about finding your way home
    for the holidays / by Max Lucado.
        p.   cm.
    ISBN 0-8499-1546-5 (hardcover). — ISBN 0-8499-6287-0 (audio)
    1. Christmas stories, American.   I. Title.
PS3562.U225S4 1998
813'.54—dc21   98-24180
                                                    CIP

Printed in Hong Kong

8 9 0 1 2 3 4 5 9 NGP 9 8 7 6 5 4 3 2 1

Dedicated to all single parents.

May God give you strength.

I lowered my windshield visor,

both to block the afternoon sun and

retrieve the photo. With one hand

holding the picture and the other on

the steering wheel, I inched my rental

car down Main Street.

Clearwater, Texas was ready for Christmas. The sky was bright winter blue. A breeze just crisp enough for a jacket swayed the large plastic bells hanging beneath the lamp lights. Aluminum garlands connected the power poles, and Frosty the Snowman chased his hat on the Dairy Kreem window. Even the pick-up truck in front of me had a wreath hanging on its tailgate. This central Texas town was ready for Christmas. But I wasn't.

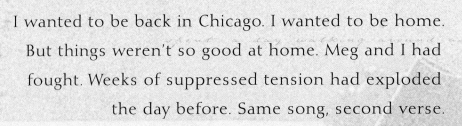

I wanted to be back in Chicago. I wanted to be home. But things weren't so good at home. Meg and I had fought. Weeks of suppressed tension had exploded the day before. Same song, second verse.

"You promised to spend more time at home," she said.

"You promised not to nag," I replied.

She says I work too much. I say we've got bills to pay. She feels neglected. I feel frustrated. Finally, she told me we needed some--what was the word? Oh yeah, we needed some "space". . . some time apart, and I agreed. I had an assignment in Dallas anyway, so why not go to Texas a few days early?

So, it was the fight with Meg that got me to Texas. But it was the photo that led me to Clearwater. My dad had received it in the mail. No return address. No letter. Just this photo: a black-and-white image of a large, stone building. I could barely make out the words on the sign in front: Clearwater Lutheran Church.

Dad had no clue what the photo meant or who had sent it. We were familiar with the town, of course. Clearwater was where I was born and adopted. But we never lived there. My only previous visit had been when I was fresh out of college and curious. I had spent a day walking around asking questions, but that was twenty years ago. I hadn't been back since. And I wouldn't have returned now except Meg needed "space" and I could use an answer about the photo.

I pulled over to the side of the road and stopped in front of a two-story brick courthouse. Cardboard cutouts of Santa and his reindeer teetered on the lawn. I lowered my window and showed the photo to a couple of aging cowboys leaning against the side of a truck.

"Ever seen this place?" I asked.

They smiled at each other
and one cowboy spoke. "If you've
got a strong arm, you could throw
a rock from here and hit it."

He instructed me to turn right
past the courthouse and turn right
again. And when I did, I saw it. The
church in the photo.

Tall elms canopied

My preconceived notion of a small-town church didn't match what I was seeing. I had always imagined a small, white-framed building with a simple belfry over the entrance. Something like an overgrown dollhouse. Not so, this structure. The white stone walls and tall steel roof spoke of permanence. Long wings extended to the right and left. I had expressed similar surprise when Dad first showed me the photo. But he had reminded me about the large number of German immigrants in the area--immigrants who took both their faith and their crafts seriously.

he wide sidewalk to the church steps

I parked in one of the diagonal spots near the church. In deference to the December chill, I put on my jacket, then grabbed my cap and gloves as I got out of the car. Tall elms canopied the wide sidewalk to the church steps. To my right was a brick sign bearing the name of the church in bronzed letters. On the left side of the church a nativity scene stood on the lawn. Although I didn't pause to examine it, I was impressed by its quality. Like the church, it seemed sturdy and detailed. I made a mental note to examine it later.

A sudden gust of wind at my back forced me to use two hands to pull open the thick wooden doors. Organ music welcomed me as I entered. With cap and gloves in hand, I stopped in the foyer. It was empty. From the look of things, it wouldn't be empty for long. The church had the appearance of a service about to happen. Large red and white poinsettias sat on the floor flanking the foyer doors. A guest book, open and ready to receive the names of visitors, rested on a podium. Garlands of pine looped across a large window that separated the foyer from the sanctuary.

I opened the doors and took a step inside. As I did, the volume of the organ music rose a notch. A long, carpeted aisle bisected the auditorium, and a vaulted ceiling rose above it. Evening sunlight, tinted red by stained glass cast long rectangles across the empty pews. An advent wreath hung on the pulpit, and unlit candles sat on the window sills. The only movements were those of a silver-haired woman rehearsing on the organ and an older fellow placing programs in hymnal racks. Neither noticed my entrance.

I spoke in the direction of the man. "Is there a service tonight?"

No response.

"IS THERE A

"Excuse me," I said a little louder, "is there a service tonight?"

He looked up at me through wire-rimmed glasses, cocked his head, and cupped a hand behind his ear.

"I said, 'Is there a Christmas service tonight?!'" I felt awkward raising my voice in the sanctuary.

"No, we don't need a linen service, thank you. We wash our own towels."

I chuckled to myself and, when I did, I noticed how good it felt and how long it'd been. "No," I repeated, walking in his direction. "I was asking about the Christmas Eve service."

SERVICE TONIGHT?"

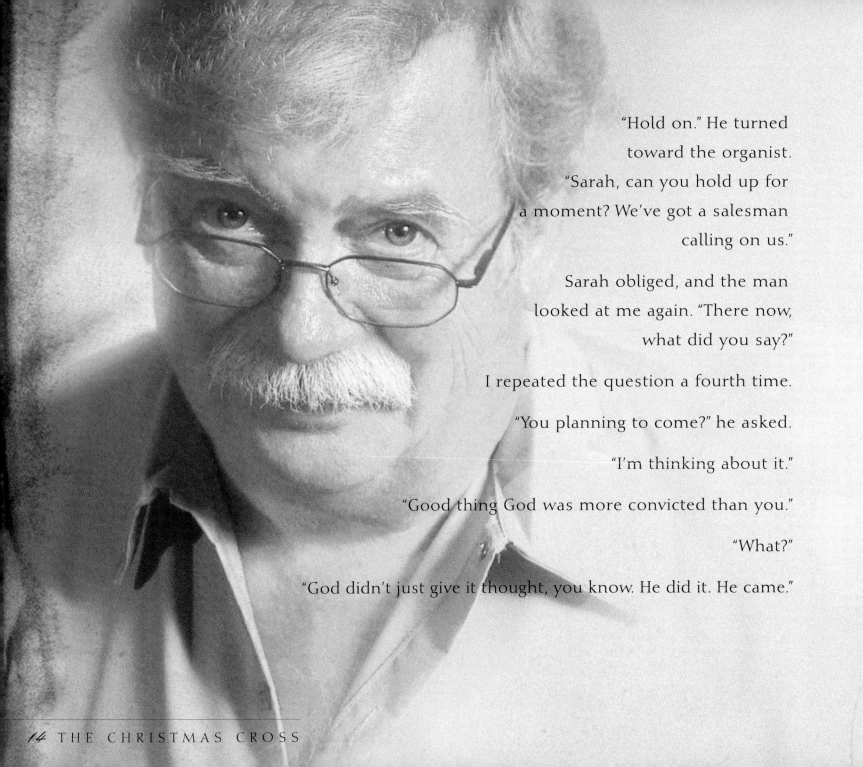

"Hold on." He turned toward the organist. "Sarah, can you hold up for a moment? We've got a salesman calling on us."

Sarah obliged, and the man looked at me again. "There now, what did you say?"

I repeated the question a fourth time.

"You planning to come?" he asked.

"I'm thinking about it."

"Good thing God was more convicted than you."

"What?"

"God didn't just give it thought, you know. He did it. He came."

Spunky, this guy.

Short and square bodied. Not fat, but barrel chested. "Maintenance" was stenciled over the pocket of his gray shirt. He stepped out from the pews, walked up the aisle, and stood in front of me. As blue eyes sized me up, his stubby fingers scratched a thick crop of white hair.

"Been a while since you've been in church?" His accent didn't sound pure Texan. Midwestern, maybe?

I suppose I wasn't cloaking my discomfort too well. It *had* been a while since I'd been in a church. And I did feel awkward being there, so I sidestepped the comment.

"I came because of this." I produced the photo. He looked down through his bifocals and smiled.

"My, the trees have grown." Looking up at me, he asked, "Where you from?"

"Chicago. I'm a journalist."

I don't always say that, but the old fellow seemed to be grading me and I felt I could use a few points. If I earned any, he didn't say.

"You ought to be home for Christmas, son."

"Well, I'd like to, but I have an assignment and . . ."

"And your work has you out of town on Christmas Eve?"

Who are you to grill me? I started to ask, but didn't. Instead, I picked up a worship program and looked at it. "Yeah, being home would be nice, but since I'm here I thought I'd . . ."

"Six o'clock."

"What?"

"The service. It starts at six." He extended a hand in my direction. "Joe's my name. Forgive me for being nosy. It's just that a man away from his wife . . ."

"How did you . . ."

"Your finger. I can see where your ring was. Must have been recent."

I looked at my hand and thumbed the line. Angry at Meg, I'd stuck my wedding band in my pocket on the plane. "Yeah, recent," I shrugged. "Listen, I'll be back at six. I'd like to meet the pastor. I've got some things to do now, though," I said, putting the program back in the hymnal rack.

Who are you to grill me?

What a lie, I mumbled to myself as I turned. I had absolutely nothing to do and nowhere to go. Joe watched me as I walked down the aisle. At least I think he did. Only when I reached the foyer did I hear him whistling and working again. As I gave the auditorium one final look, Sarah resumed her rehearsal. I turned to go outside. The wooden doors were still stubborn. I paused on the steps, put on my cap, and looked around.

Several people stepped into the corner drugstore. Last-minute shoppers, I thought. A fellow with a western hat gave me a wave as he walked past. Not far behind him a woman clutching a shopping bag of gifts in one hand and a youngster's hand in the other scurried into the Smart Shoppe across the street. In the adjacent lot, cars encircled Happy's Cafe. Through snow-painted windows I could see families at the tables. I sighed at the sight of them, struck by the irony of my plight. *All alone forty years ago. All alone, today.*

I took a deep breath and started down the steps, again noticing the manger scene to my right. Curious, I headed toward it, the yellow grass cracking beneath my feet as I walked.

Lowering my head, I entered the stable and studied the figures, obviously hand-carved, hand-painted. They were the largest ones I'd seen. The shepherds, though kneeling, were over two-feet tall. I was struck by the extraordinary detail of the carvings. Joseph's beard wasn't just painted on; it was carved into the wood. His hand, resting on the manger, was complete with knuckles and fingernails. Mary knelt on the other side, her hand brushing hair back from her forehead as she looked at her son. One shepherd had his hand on the shoulder of another. Their faces had a leather hue and a convincing look of awe. Even the wise men were unique, one gesturing at the infant, another holding the bridle of a camel, and the third reverently placing a gift before the crib.

Two cows dozed on folded legs. A sheep and three lambs occupied the space on the other side. I bent down and ran my hand over the white, varnished back of the smallest lamb.

"You won't find a set like this anywhere."

A SET

Startled, I stood and bumped my head of the roof of the stable. I turned. It was Joe. He'd donned a baseball cap and jacket.

"Each figure hand-carved," he continued, "right down to the last eyelash and hoof. Mr. Ottolman donated the manger scene to the church. It's been the pride of the city ever since."

"Mr. Autobahn?" I asked.

"Ottolman. A woodworker from Germany. This was his penance."

"Penance?"

"Self-imposed. He was drunk the night his wife went into labor. So drunk he wrecked the car while driving her to the hospital. The baby survived, but the mother didn't make it."

You won't find LIKE THIS ANYWHERE

I squatted down and put my hand on Mary's face.
I could feel the individual hairs of her eyebrows. Then I ran
my finger across the smile on her lips.

"He spent the better part of a decade doing the work.
He made a living building furniture and spent his time raising
Carmen and carving these figures."

"Carmen was his daughter?"

"Yes, the girl who survived. Let me show you something."
Joe removed his hat, either out of reverence for the crèche
or regard for the low roof, and knelt before the crib. I joined
him. The grass was cold beneath our knees.

"Pull the blanket off the infant Jesus and look at his chest."

I did as he asked.

Evening shadows made it difficult to see, but I could make out the figure of a small cross furrowed into the wood. I ran my finger over the groove. Maybe a couple of inches long and half that wide; deep and wide enough for the tip of my finger.

"For nearly ten years a wooden scarlet cross sat in that space."

the blanket off

He could see the question on my face and explained. "Ottolman wasn't a believer when he began. But something about carving the face of the Messiah . . ." His voice drifted off for a minute as he touched the tiny chin. "Somewhere in the process he became interested. He went to church, this very church, and asked the pastor all about Jesus. Reverend Jackson told him not just about the birth but about the death of Christ and invited him to Sunday worship. He went.

"He took little Carmen with him. She was only a toddler. The two sat on the front pew and heard their first sermon. 'Born Crucified' was the name of the lesson. The message changed his life. He told everyone about it."

Joe smiled and stepped out from under the roof, then stood in the grass, his breath puffing clouds in the cold.

born with love in
Crucified
and the cross in his heart

"He used to retell the message to Carmen every night. He'd sit her on her bed and pretend he was the pastor." At this point Joe lowered his voice and took on a pulpit rhythm. "'Baby Jesus was born to be crucified. He came not just for Bethlehem but for Calvary—not just to live with us, but to die for us. Born with love in his eyes and the cross in his heart. He was born crucified.'"

Joe's blue eyes blazed and his meaty fist punched the air, as if he were the reverend making the point.

"So you knew him?"

"I did."

"And Carmen?"

"Yes," he sighed. "Very well."

Still on my knees, I turned back to the baby and touched the indentation left by the cross. He chuckled behind me and said, "Ottolman told some of the members about his idea for the carving and they thought it was crazy. 'Baby Jesus doesn't wear a cross,' they said. But he insisted. And one Christmas when he brought the figures out and set them on the lawn, there was a wooden scarlet cross in the baby's chest. Some people made a stink about it, but the reverend, he didn't mind."

"And the cross, where is it now? Is it lost?"

Joe put his hands in his pockets and stared off into space, then looked back at me. "No, it's not lost. Come with me." He turned and walked toward the church doors. I followed him into the building.

"Over here," he called as I stood in the entrance, letting my eyes adjust to the darkening room.

I took off my cap, and Joe led me through a door off the right side of the foyer, down a long hall. We passed a row of portraits, apparently a gallery of pastors. I followed him around a corner until we stood in front of a door marked "Library." There must have been thirty keys hanging from a chain on Joe's belt. One of them unlocked the door. After he turned on the lights, we crossed the room to a corner where a stand held a thick scrapbook. In a couple of turns the old man found what he was looking for.

"This article appeared in our paper on Christmas Day, 1958."

The yellowed newsprint told the story:

Stolen Baby Jesus Home for Christmas

He was silent as I read the first paragraph:

Christmas Day

"Mr. Ottolman must have been pretty angry."

"No, he wasn't upset."

"But his baby was taken."

"Finish the article, and I'll get us some coffee."

As he left the room, I continued reading:

The baby Jesus, part of a set hand-carved by a local woodworker, was taken from the Clearwater Lutheran Church sometime yesterday. The minister had posted a sign pleading for the babe's return. "At last night's Christmas Eve service," Reverend Jackson reported, "we had special prayers for the baby. With the homecoming of Baby Jesus, the prayers were answered."

I was staring at the photograph attached to the article when Joe returned with two Styrofoam cups of coffee. "Look closely," he said. "See anything missing?"

"The cross?"

Joe nodded. "Won't you sit down?"

We sat on either side of a long mahogany table. Joe took a sip of coffee and began.

Nineteen fifty-eight

"Nineteen fifty-eight. Carmen was eighteen. Lively, lovely girl, she was. Ottolman did his best to raise her but she had her own ways. Would have been good had he remarried, but he never did.

"Told people a man only has room in his heart for one woman; Carmen was his. She was everything to him. Took her fishing on Saturdays and picked her up after school. Every Sunday the two sat on the front pew of this church and sang. My how they sang.

"And every night he would pray. He'd thank God for his good grace and then beg God, 'Take care of my Carmen, Lord. Take care of my Carmen.'"

Joe looked away as if remembering her. For the first time I heard conversation in the hall. Parishioners were beginning to arrive. Somewhere a choir was rehearsing. Just as I found myself hoping Joe wouldn't stop his story, he continued. "Carmen's mother was a beauty from Mexico. And Carmen had every ounce of her beauty. Dark skin, black hair, and eyes that could melt your soul. She couldn't walk down Main Street without being whistled at.

TAKE CARE OF MY

"This bothered Ottolman. He was from the old school, you know. As she got older, he got stricter. It was for her own good, but she couldn't see that. He went too far, Ottolman did. He went too far. Told her to stay away from boys and to stay away from anyplace where boys were. And she did, mostly.

CARMEN, LORD

"Early in the summer of 'fifty-eight, Carmen discovered she was pregnant. She kept it from her father as long as she could. Being small of stature, she hid it quite well. But by December it was obvious. When he found out, he did something very, very bad. For the rest of his life he regretted that December night."

Joe's tone shifted from one of telling to one of questioning. "Why do people do the thing they swear they'll never do?" I wasn't sure if he expected me to answer or not, but before I could, he sighed and continued.

"Well, Carmen's dad got mad and he got drunk. He wasn't a bad man; he just did a bad thing. He forgot his faith. And . . ." Joe shook his head, "you're not going to believe this. Just before Christmas, he and Carmen had a wreck. Twice in one lifetime the man wrecked a car carrying the woman he loved."

Joe stopped again, I suppose to let me mull over what he'd said. He was right; I found it hard to believe. How could a man repeat such a tragic event? But then, it occurred to me that I was doing the same with Meg. Swearing to do better, only to fail again . . . and again. Maybe it wasn't so impossible after all.

"Go on," I urged. "What happened to them?"

"Ottolman came out of it OK, but Carmen was hurt, badly hurt. They took her to the hospital where her daddy sat by her bed every single minute. 'Oh, Jesus,' he would pray, 'take care of my Carmen. Don't let her die.' The doctors told him they would have to take the baby as soon as Carmen was stable.

TWICE IN ONE

"The night passed and Carmen slept. Ottolman sat by her side and Carmen slept. She slept right up until Christmas Eve morning. Then she woke up. Her first words were a question: 'Daddy, has my baby come?'

"He bounded out of his chair and took her hand. 'No, Carmen, but the baby is fine. The doctors are sure the baby is fine.'

"'Where am I?'

"He knelt at her bedside. 'You're in the hospital, darling. It's Christmas Eve.' He put her hand on his cheek and told her what had happened. He told her about his drinking and the accident and he began to weep. 'I'm so sorry, Carmen. I'm so sorry.'

"Then Carmen did a wonderful thing. She stroked her father's head and said, 'It's OK, Papa. It's OK. I love you.'

"He leaned forward and put his face in the crook of her neck and wept. Carmen cried, too. She put her arm around her daddy's neck and cried.

"Neither said anything for the longest time; they just held each other, each tear washing away the hurt. Finally Carmen spoke: 'Papa, will the baby come before Christmas?'

"'I don't know, princess.'"

"'I'd like that.' She smiled, her brown eyes twinkling. 'I'd like very much to have a baby to hold this Christmas Eve.'

"Those were her final words. She closed her eyes to rest. But she never woke up."

Joe's eyes misted and he looked at the floor. I started to say he didn't have to tell me the rest of the story, but when he lifted his head, he was smiling—a soft, tender smile. "It was around lunchtime when Ottolman had the idea. 'You want to sleep with your baby, Carmen?' he whispered in her ear. 'I'll get you your baby.'

'I'll get you your baby.'

'I'll get you your baby.'

"For the first time in weeks he left the hospital. Out the door and across the street he marched. He walked straight past the courthouse and slowed his pace only when he neared the church. For a long time he stared at the crèche from across the street— the very crèche you saw this afternoon. He was planning something. He took a deep breath and crossed the church lawn.

"He began adjusting the manger scene, like he was inspecting the figures, looking for cracks or marks. Anyone passing by would have thought nothing of Mr. Ottolman examining his handiwork. And no one passing by would have seen that when he left, there was no baby Jesus in the manger.

"Only an hour later, when the reverend was showing the display to his grandchildren, did anyone notice. By then, the baby with the scarlet cross was wrapped in a blanket and nestled under the covers next to Carmen.

"Her final wish was granted. She held a baby on Christmas Eve."

"For a long time neither Joe nor I spoke. He sat leaning forward, hands folded between his knees. He wasn't here. Nor was I. We were both in the world of Ottolman and Carmen and the sculptured baby in the manger. Though I'd never seen their faces, I could see them in my mind. I could see Ottolman pulling back the hospital sheets and placing the infant Jesus next to his daughter. And I could see him setting a chair next to the bed, taking Carmen's hand in his . . . and waiting.

I broke the silence with one word: "Carmen?"

"She died two days later."

"The baby?"

"He came, early. But he came."

"Mr. Ottolman?"

"He stayed on in Clearwater. Still lives here, as a matter of fact. But he never went back to his house. He couldn't face the emptiness."

"So what happened to him?"

Joe cleared his throat. "Well, the church took him in—gave him a job and a little room at the back of the sanctuary."

"Who are you?"

Until that moment, until he spoke those words, the possibility had not entered my mind. I leaned forward and looked directly into his face.

"Who *are* you?"

"You have her eyes, you know," he whispered.

"You mean, Carmen was . . ."

"Yes. Your mother. And I'm, well, I'm . . . your . . ."

". . . Grandfather?"

His chin began to tremble as he told me, "I've made some big mistakes, son. And I pray I'm not making another one right now. I just wanted you to know what happened. And I wanted to see you while I still could."

As I struggled to understand, he reached into his shirt pocket. He removed an object, placed it in my palm, and folded my hand around it. "I've been keeping this for you. She would want you to have it." And I opened my hand to see a cross—a small, wooden, scarlet cross.

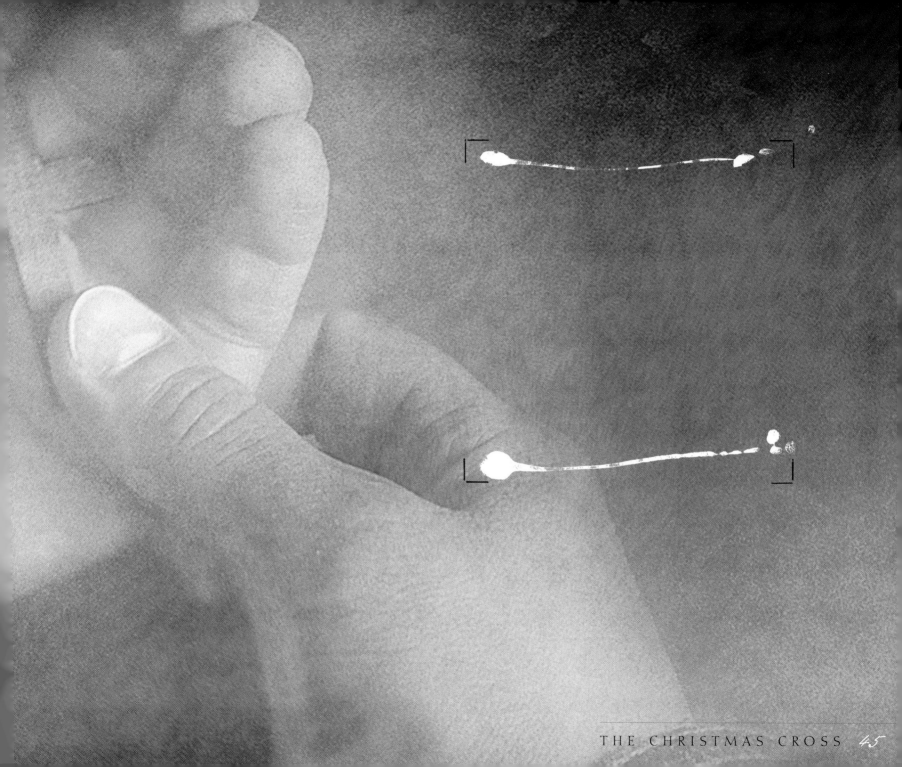

Later that evening I called Meg from my room. I told her about Carmen, Ottolman, and the family I'd discovered. "Were you angry at Joe?" she asked.

"Funny," I said, "of all the emotions that flooded me in that church library, anger wasn't one of them. Shock? Yes. Disbelief? Of course. But anger, no. Joe's assessment of himself sounds fair. He is a good man who did a very bad thing."

So Meg flew to Texas to be with us.

She made it to Clearwater in time to have dinner with two men who, by virtue of mistakes and mercy and Christmas miracles, had found their way home for the holidays.

There was a long pause. Meg and I both knew what needed to be discussed next. She found a way to broach it. "What about me?" Her voice was soft. "Are you angry at me?"

With no hesitation, I responded, "No, there's been too much anger between us."

She agreed. "If Carmen forgave Joe, don't you suppose we could do the same for each other?"

"I'll be home tomorrow," I told my wife.

"I've got a better idea," she replied.

"Are you angry at me?"